My Himalayan Journey

A Spiritual and Physical Trek to Shrikhand Mahadev Kailash

TRAVELOVER
MITHUN ANANTHAKRISHNAN
Om Namah Shivaya

This travel memoir is dedicated to my beloved
Hima, Omshiv, Omsvah, Dad, Mom and Mummy

To my Spiritual Guru
Dasji
&
to my dear
Radhakrishnanji and Balakrishnanji
&
to my friends from the mountains

Heartfelt thanks to my mentor
Rahul Nandan (Author & Journalist)

CONTENTS

LEGEND

LEGEND

In the mystic Himalayas, a demon named Bhasmasur sought immense power and immortality. Pleased by his devotion, Lord Shiva granted him the ability to turn anyone he touched into ashes. But Bhasmasur, drunk on power, attempted to destroy Shiva himself. To escape, Shiva fled to a cave high in the mountains, meditating in deep Samadhi on a 75-foot stone Shivling, 16,900 feet above sea level.

Meanwhile, Lord Vishnu, in the form of the enchanting Mohini, tricked Bhasmasur into turning himself to ashes. Yet, Shiva remained in his profound meditation, untouched by the world. Moved by his unwavering devotion, Goddess Parvati wept, filling Nayana Sarovar Lake with her tears. Her sorrowful devotion awakened Shiva, causing the Shivling to shatter and the mountain to be named Shrikhand Mahadev Kailash.

The mountain became a sacred pilgrimage site, attracting devotees, including the Pandavas during their exile. Shrikhand Mahadev stands today as a symbol of divine power, devotion, and the eternal connection between the gods and the earth.

Let's open the pages of this journey and begin the
Travel Memoir

A Journey Begins
Trials, Triumphs, and the Road to Shrikhand Mahadev

The alarm rings at 5 a.m. on September 27, 2023. But before diving into the day's adventure, let me introduce myself. I am a Mechanical Engineer living in Bangalore, originally from Kerala, "God's Own Country." I share my life with my wonderful wife and two amazing sons. Together, we cherish the serenity of nature's embrace. To challenge my physical limits and reconnect with the raw beauty of the world, I often journey to remote corners of the Himalayas.

That morning, I began my journey from my apartment in Bangalore at 5:45 a.m., taking a cab to Bangalore Cantonment to pick up Dasji and RKji—my mentors and fellow travelers. I've written about Dasji before in my book Panchkedar and Badrinath. To put it simply, he serves as a bridge between me and Lord Shiva.

After a quick breakfast stop en route to Bangalore International Airport, I began my fast, preparing my body for the grueling trek ahead. We arrived at the airport by 9 a.m., and after clearing security, the chaos of travel began. There's always something, isn't there? The first mishap: RKji couldn't find his Aadhaar card. It was one of those moments, like searching for your glasses only to find them on your head. After a few frantic runs and complaints, he found it in his purse. But that was just the beginning—next, we were informed we couldn't carry our backup trek batteries for our headlights.

A Malayalam proverb says, "Onnil thottal moonu" (if one issue arises, there will be two more). We prayed to Shivji that our third issue be a minor one. With our flight scheduled for 11:30 a.m., we had plenty of time after clearing security. Dasji and RKji began chanting mantras, while I wandered off to find a lounge where I could use my international bank cards for a free meal. I settled for fruit to stay hydrated.

The flight took off on time at 11:30 a.m., and by 2:30 p.m., we landed in Chandigarh. I had bought a GoPro for Dasji in Bangalore, which I was carrying along with my cabin bag. And, as the fates would have it, I left the camera on the aircraft. Unlike the earlier issues, this felt more serious. But Dasji, ever composed, helped us retrieve the camera with the assistance of an airline ground staff member. Three hurdles down, we felt relieved, and the superstition was finally behind us.

In Chandigarh, we met our dear friend Balakrishnanji, a successful businessman from Chennai who had joined us for the Shrikhand Mahadev Kailash trek. Our guide, Kisan, from Ghalincha Village, picked us up. Chandigarh, a city shared by two states, welcomed us with signs from both, a rare sight indeed.

We stopped for tea in Kalka, and as fate would have it, the tea spilled onto Balakrishnaji's phone. Once again, the Malayalam proverb held true, and we laughed together at the day's mishaps over our tea. The journey continued through narrow, hilly roads, traffic jams, and even a punctured tire. Originally, we planned to stay in Kufri, but later chose Piyush Residency in Narkhanda, a place famous for its apples. A warm vegetarian soup awaited us before we turned in for the night.

It was only day one, but already the adventure had begun in full force.

Blessings of the Peaks
From Temples to Apple Orchards

The bright morning sun streamed through the windows, greeting us with a majestic view of the Himalayan peaks. In these highlands, dogs are called Bhairavas, a reincarnation of Lord Shiva, and feeding them is considered a sacred act. Kisan, our guide, had suggested stopping at Narkhanda to visit the Hatu Mata Temple and seek her blessings for our trek. As we entered, we saw the priest engrossed in chanting mantras, so deeply immersed that he didn't notice us sitting before the sanctum. The temple's unique feature was its view of two Kailash peaks—Kinnaur and Shrikhand Kailash—an unforgettable sight, both mesmerizing and daunting, as it reminded us of the challenge that lay ahead.

Realizing that network reception would be scarce as we moved forward, we decided to have a group call with our families. Kisan then took us on a detour to visit the Hanuman and Durga Devi temples in Rampur. Himachal, known for its apples, blessed us with an apple Prasada from the temple. Kisan had also brought apples from his village, which provided a welcome refreshment.

The Sutlej River, flowing alongside our drive, offered a picturesque view, and Kisan used a small waterfall to clean our car. We made a quick stop at Nirmand to buy vegetables and groceries, where the locals warned us that the weather was unsuitable for the Shrikhand trek. Their warnings gave us pause, but Dasji remained calm, offering us the strength to push forward. Balakrishnanji reassured us that we shouldn't let the locals' concerns cause unnecessary anxiety.

Kisan continued driving, stopping at Bagipul to pick up some final supplies. By 2:50 p.m., we reached Jaon Village, the base for the Shrikhand Mahadev Kailash trek. We stayed in a homestay nestled among apple orchards, where we could pick fresh apples straight from the trees. Kisan advised us to pre—

-pare our trekking bags, and we met fellow trekkers staying at the same homestay, sharing stories and exchanging words of encouragement.

Before the evening chanting, we took a refreshing shower and witnessed a surreal sight—the moon rising and setting behind the mountains at such a rapid pace, it felt like watching a timelapse video. The moon, a pearl in the vast black sea, made us feel truly blessed to witness its beauty.

The Trek Begins
Trail Angels and Steep Ascents

This day marked the beginning of one of India's most demanding treks. We rose at 4:30 a.m., ready to embark on the journey ahead. Allow me to introduce our companions— the pahadis (mountain folk) from Galincha village, who are cousins of our lead guide, Kisan. Having arrived on foot from Galincha the day before, they embody the belief that walking is both the healthiest and quickest way to navigate the hills. Our team included Lalith (Lalli), Ome Thakur, Chetan, Devaraj, Deepan, Yogi, Mori, and Gopal. These trail angels would support us by carrying our larger backpacks, providing food and shelter, and ensuring our comfort throughout the trek. We carried smaller backpacks and hiking sticks, with each of us assigned a companion: Lalli was assigned to me, Devaraj to Dasji, Deepan to Balakrishnanji, Yogi to RKji, and the rest handled groceries, vegetables, and packed food to keep our hunger at bay. Being from God's Own Country, we carried rice porridge and homemade snacks, such as kondattam, as our sustenance.

At the outset of our trek, we met the Jaonis, native villagers whose lives revolve around apples and livestock. As we made our way forward, our first break came after an hour and a half of trekking at Singhad, where a government-run trekking shelter is located. The trekking season for Shrikhand Mahadev Kailash was closed during our visit, so the shelter was shut, awaiting the next season. We stopped for breakfast at Bahrati Nala (7,283 ft), where we met a Babaji, a phalahari (someone who lives solely on fruits). The rhythmic sound of the pounding water was mesmerizing, almost as if it could freeze time itself. After offering our prayers and taking a much-needed rest, we continued the steep ascent up Dandi-Dhar.

As we climbed, everyone moved at their own pace. I felt a—

deep connection with Lalli, as if he had been my brother in a past life. Sometimes, the people we meet in life come with an unexplainable, divine bond. Our thoughts on life seemed to align effortlessly, and his presence distracted me from the toll the steep ascent was taking on my knee. We were climbing from 6,000 ft to 11,500 ft through the rugged Devdar forest— gruelling, steep, and unforgiving. But with Lalli by my side, I found myself moving forward without consciously thinking about it.

After reaching Thachru, we had a choice to continue or return. This moment was critical, as it's at Thachru that one can catch the first glimpse of Shrikhand Mahadev. Many pilgrims choose to turn back from here after seeing Mahadev, but we decided to press on. Our early-arrival companions had already set up tents for the day and began preparing rice porridge for dinner. Inside the tent, as we chatted, I offered coconut barfi—my mother's sweet delicacy—to the fellow trekkers, who eagerly enjoyed it.

We bundled up against the cold, had a warm meal, and listened to Kisan, who vowed to guide us all to the summit. With that, we finally surrendered to the heavy pull of sleep, knowing that tomorrow would bring us one step closer to our goal.

Battling the Elements
Hailstorms and Frozen Waterfalls

The soft drizzling of rain on the tent that morning wasn't exactly a welcoming sound. At 5 a.m., I felt a numbing cold in my little and ring fingers, a reminder of the frigid temperatures. The strain in my back from yesterday's grueling seven-hour climb up a 70-degree incline was palpable, yet the trek must go on. I forced myself to rise and started moving at 7:15 a.m.

By 9 a.m., we reached Kali Top, trudging through rugged terrain. The place greeted us with a hailstorm, a surreal and unforgettable experience that only heightened the majesty of the scene. Dasji reached the Kali top summit first, followed by me, then RKji and BKji. I should mention that both RKji and BKji are over 60, but their endurance and will to conquer this trek were nothing short of remarkable. Despite their age, they had already surpassed Tachru and were determined to push on.

So, Dasji and I waited for them to join us at Kali Top, believed to be the residence of Goddess Kali. The sight that greeted us was breathtaking—a rainbow stretching across the entire mountain, its colors vibrant against the sky. We spent some time there, snapping photos and taking a much-needed break. The area was teeming with rich flora and fauna, and our guides shared some medicinal herbs and fruits that revitalized us, offering a burst of energy in the bleak weather.

By 12:45 p.m., we arrived at our tent in Kunsa. Our progress had been much better than the previous day, and although the weather had been challenging, we had pushed forward. But our guide had advised that we should rest here for the day, as sudden elevation changes can be dangerous. Most of the other trekkers had already passed Kunsa, but when I spoke to Dasji about it, he reminded me that we weren't seasoned professionals. As always, he was right. We were in the hills,—

and his insights were spot on. So, we decided to follow his advice and rest for the day, grateful for his wisdom and the safety it ensured.

Rainbow arching over the majestic Himalayas

Whispers of the Summit

A Journey of Belief and Devotion

It was a day that held special meaning for me. As we trekked higher into the majestic Himalayas, I found myself reflecting on how I could make this day unforgettable for my wife, even from such a distance. Then, by sheer luck, I got a phone signal. Without hesitation, I set up a video call, and the entire team, with the stunning Himalayan backdrop, wished her a heartfelt happy birthday. I knew that the little things brought her joy, and this moment would surely light up her day, but I wanted to do more. Yet, I put that thought aside for the time being, as a monumental task lay ahead of us.

We took breaks along the way, stopping for lunch in Bheem Dhwari at 10:30 a.m. The sun blazed brightly above us, and we ate oats, sharing stories and laughter. It was a reminder that, as the world says, we Indians are united in our diversity. Dasji, always the first to start chanting, led the way as we continued our ascent. We paused by a waterfall to chant together, and I could sense that the summit was nearing.

By 1:45 p.m., we reached Paravati Bagh, a place that felt like the very heart of heaven—a realm where delusions and beliefs danced together. In that tranquil, detached air, I couldn't resist calling my parents, wife, and children for a virtual darshan of the summit. They too witnessed the awe-inspiring view of Shrikhand Mahadev, even from afar.

The weather on the hills, as always, was unpredictable—sun, rain, and hailstorms came in quick succession. But we were greeted by the breathtaking sight of Brahmakamal, a flower steeped in sacred symbolism. It is said that Lord Brahma created this mystical flower to help Lord Shiva place an elephant's head on Lord Ganesh's body. In its presence, we were overwhelmed with a mixture of awe, reverence, and a deep sense of belief as we anxiously awaited the final push to the summit the next day.

As I settled in for the night, I couldn't recall exactly when I drifted off, but I remember feeling a deep sense of peace, as if Lord Shiva himself had whispered in my ear: "Give me your problems and slumber; I will make a way for you. I did it before, and I will do it again."

The Ascent to Shrikhand Mahadev
Tears and Triumph

The moment we had all set out for was finally upon us. At 2:00 a.m., we geared up, strapped on our trekking headlights, and began our ascent into the darkness. Everything felt surreal. Beyond Parvati Bagh, there was no longer any grassland—only moraines and snow lay ahead. With the darkness enveloping us, we could hardly see more than a few feet in front and moved at our own pace, taking cautious steps toward the unknown.

According to Hindu mythology, when Goddess Parvati waited in vain for Lord Shiva, her tears fell and formed a lake—Nayana Sarovar. Pilgrims often bathe here to receive her blessings, but at this time of year, with the temperature hovering around -8°C, a bath was out of the question. We spent a few moments at the lake, feeling an overwhelming sense of divinity in the air. The place felt both eerie and sacred, its vibrations so intense that it felt as though the very land had the power to possess us.

As we trudged on, crossing snow and navigating giant boulders, our energy slowly drained. Seven peaks stood between us and the summit, and the air grew thinner with every step, each one more laborious than the last. The snow sank beneath our feet, making progress feel impossible. Yet, after hours of relentless effort, we finally reached the summit.

Overcome with emotion, I wept like a child. Was it the divine presence in the air, or the culmination of this grueling journey that brought tears to my eyes? I looked around and saw that I wasn't alone—everyone was shedding tears at the summit. The snowstorm howled around us, the winds whipping fiercely, but there was an undeniable sense of oneness and transcendence that filled me with a boundless energy, despite the bleak weather.

Dasji, too, was moved, and we embraced, both of us lost in—

eternal joy. Slowly, we began to regain awareness of where we were. In front of us stood Shrikhand Mahadev, a massive 75-foot stone resembling the face of Hanumanji. We knelt before it, lit camphor, and offered our thanks to the Lord for granting us the strength to reach this holy place.

Our guide, Kisan, soon reminded us of the worsening weather and urged us to descend immediately. We learned that RKji, one of our fellow trekkers, had been unable to continue to the summit and had turned back. BKji, too, had decided to stop at Nayana Sarovar, feeling uneasy.

After a few photographs, Dasji and I began our descent. The snow was now knee-deep, and we had to tread carefully, unsure of how deep the drifts were. My feet were numb from the snow seeping into my boots, but there was no time to stop. After clearing the snow from my boots on a nearby rock, we continued our descent, relieved when the sun broke through, warming our frozen feet.

We made our way back to the safer zones, and I allowed myself a moment to celebrate this monumental achievement. My companions—my angel trekkers—stood with me, and together we captured some of the most breathtaking pictures. A thought crossed my mind: how wonderful it would have been for my wife and kids to witness this. In that moment, I decided to create a special memory for her. I wrote "Happy Birthday Hima" in the snow and posed beside it. Lalli took a picture, and I imagined her joy as she saw it.

We stopped again at Nayana Sarovar, meditated, and drank the holy water before taking a detour to see the ever-beautiful Brahmakamal. Afterward, we returned to the tent, greeted by warmth and camaraderie. Kisan shared the temperatures recorded during our climb: -3°C at Parvati Bagh when we started at 2 a.m., -8°C at Nayana Sarovar, and a chilling——

-16°C at the summit. I felt a deep sense of relief—we were fortunate to have made it back safely, as this trek has claimed many lives.

Dinner was light, and I wrapped myself in layers of blankets as the weather worsened, rain beginning to fall. With half a day to spare before we slept, I noticed RKji looking a little disheartened. When I asked him what was bothering him, he revealed that he was upset about not making it to the summit. Dasji and I sat with him, explaining how treacherous the conditions had been on our way up and how dangerous it could have been to continue downhill in such conditions, especially at his age. He had nearly completed three-fourths of the journey, but we reassured him that it was the final stretch that would test us all. Reluctantly, he agreed, although he still seemed unconvinced. I asked him what truly bothered him, and he confessed that he had a "do or die" mentality, driven by an intense love for Lord Shiva. We were left speechless by his devotion. As the day went on, his demeanor softened, and he became more at peace with the decision.

That night, I ate with a sense of contentment, finally allowing myself to relax. Wrapped in warmth, I had the best sleep of the journey, knowing that we had triumphed over the Himalayas, together.

Nayana Sarovar

HIMA
HAPPY BDAY

At the summit of Shrikhand Mahadev, a rush of reverence and achievement enveloped me, as if the divine had whispered its blessing.

Descending with Gratitude
Reflections and Revelations on the Way Back

I woke up at 4 a.m., the cold biting at my skin as I checked the temperature on my phone—it was -7°C. Even after the immense achievement of reaching the summit, I couldn't find a restful sleep. The cold and the low oxygen levels kept me tossing and turning. I huddled under a multilayer blanket for hours, trying to find warmth. By 7 a.m., the temperature had dropped to -2°C, and I could feel the chill seep into my bones. Kisan and the team were already packing the blankets, rations, and gear, preparing everything for the next trekking season, moving it to a dug-out ground.

At 8:30 a.m., we began our descent, starting our trek back to Bheem Dhwari. By 9:30 a.m., we reached our breakfast stop, where the mood was lighter. But one thing was clear: the trek isn't truly successful until we safely return to the base. Dasji, as always, led the way, taking charge and setting the pace. I stayed with RKji and BKji, enjoying a more leisurely walk, stopping frequently to capture the breathtaking peaks in the distance.

By 2:30 p.m., we arrived in Kunsa and were treated to the most comforting meal—curd rice. The atmosphere in the tent had lightened. Laughter filled the air as everyone shared stories and joked around. Despite the growing camaraderie, the weather remained unforgiving, and the cold persisted. Yet, when the sun made a rare and feeble appearance, RKji and BKji seized the opportunity to clean themselves in a small spring near the tent—an act that felt almost absurd, but necessary for their spirits.

The next morning, the cold showed no mercy. We woke up at 6:30 a.m., the chill still cutting through the air. But Dasji, inexplicably, wasn't shivering like the rest of us. We teased him, joking that he must be a cold-blooded creature. Kisan and the team packed everything up and buried the remaining supplies underground for the next season. Our next stop was Bheem Thalai. We took a breath and waited for the rest of the team to join us. The pahadis, as always, had their local music playing. Their infectious energy got the best of us, and before long, we found ourselves swept up in a dance. We laughed and bonded, a shared experience that deepened our connection with these mountain people.

The trek had mostly been downhill up to this point, but now we faced the steep ascent to Kali Top. Lalli, ever the guide, took me along a less-traveled path through large boulders, a risky but clever shortcut that saved us about 30 minutes. As we climbed, I couldn't help but shed tears in reverence to Goddess Kali, thanking her for the divine strength she had bestowed upon me.

As we walked, I heard the angel trekkers sing a folk song. Lalli taught me the lyrics, and the tune seemed to resonate deeply with me: "Shiv Kailose ke Wasi." The melody touched my soul, and I found myself lost in its simplicity and beauty. By 2 p.m., we reached Tachru, a crucial point in the trek. Locals say that if you return to Tachru after reaching the summit, your success is nearly guaranteed. To mark this accomplishment, Kisan and the team set up a bonfire, and we celebrated with warmth and stories.

Lalli and I sat by the fire, sharing personal stories and reflecting on life. Our bond grew stronger, and I felt a deep connection to him. He was young, but his maturity was far beyond his years. I found myself learning valuable life lessons from him—wisdom that can only come from the heart of the Himalayas.

We continued our descent and arrived at Bahrati Nala at 10:30 a.m., the place where we had met the phalahari sage on our way up. After breakfast, one of our trekkers, Gopal, —

began recounting stories from his previous trekking experiences. His words resonated with me: "Be satisfied with the Lord's decisions. The Lord knows us better than we know ourselves."

By 1:30 p.m., we finally reached our base camp in Jaon. After eight days without a proper wash, I had my first head bath, feeling completely rejuvenated and refreshed. The warmth of the shower was like a new life, and we sat down to a satisfying lunch. The mood was light, the sense of achievement palpable.

As we descended further, Kisan suggested we visit his village, a chance to experience the pahadi way of life up close. At first, I thought of seeing my wife and kids as soon as possible, but when Kisan presented this idea, I couldn't help but agree. We owed so much to him and his team for the unwavering support they had given us throughout this journey. Their hospitality and strength had helped us achieve what once seemed impossible.

This trek, this journey, was about more than just reaching the summit—it was about the people we met, the lessons we learned, and the bonds we forged along the way. And as I thought about it, I realized that in some strange, inexplicable way, the mountains had become a part of me.

The Warmth of Galincha
Embracing Simplicity and Connection

We set out for Kisan's village, Galincha, at 4:30 p.m. The journey began with four of us in a car and the trekkers in a small pickup truck. As we passed through the quaint village of Bagipul, we were introduced to more Hansraj folk songs. The rhythmic beats and lively tunes instantly grabbed our attention. The atmosphere was infectious, and soon enough, we were all swaying to the music, the wheels of the car rolling in time with the melody.

Our first stop was Nirmand, where we bought traditional Kinnaur-style caps, a signature piece of Kullu pahadi wear. Kisan, in the spirit of "Atithi Devo Bhava" (the guest is God), generously purchased a few more things for us, always thinking of others. We tried some local delicacies and sweets, buying some for Kisan's family as a token of our gratitude.

Next, we detoured to Devadhang, where we saw the cave (gufa) through which Lord Shiva is said to have escaped from the demon Bhasmasur to Shrikhand Peak. According to locals, the trek isn't truly complete until you visit Devadhang. The priest at the site shared the legend of Shrikhand Mahadev, explaining the deep spiritual significance of the place. Feeling inspired, we decided to reward our trekking companions. I handed Lalli some money, telling him to buy something for his sister's birthday, and his grin made my heart swell with joy.

We continued on to Singhapur for dinner, and I was struck by a simple, yet profound observation: while most of the restaurants in these places didn't look pristine, their serving plates were spotless, and the food was nothing short of delicious. It was a reminder not to judge by appearances—the people here, like their food, were warm and genuine. The mountains had a way of stripping away pretension and revealing the truth. After a long drive, we finally arrived in—

Bhathad at 1:30 a.m., running on fumes. I don't even remember when I fell asleep, exhaustion taking over in an instant.

The next morning, we woke at 7 a.m. to a beautiful sight—Kisan's two daughters and their cousins, faces glowing with warmth and innocence. The villages surrounding us—Galincha, Mesyar, Majalli, and Kempeda—took root in our hearts. Galincha, Kisan's home, is a picturesque village where the locals make their living through apple farming and livestock. We were welcomed into Kisan's vibrant home, a colorful building with wooden rooms that provided shelter from the biting cold.

The hospitality was extraordinary. We were treated to the best drink in the world—the milk of their livestock. There was nothing quite like it. Ome and Devaraj, part of the local community, took us on a tour of the village, which is nestled in a mountain valley. Unlike cities where neighbors barely know each other, here, everyone is connected, sharing a sense of community and belonging. The bonds were deep, and the love between people was palpable. Even more humbling was how happy they seemed with so little. In places like this, basic needs were a luxury, and yet, the people lived in harmony, with a contentment that many of us in cities rarely experience. Later, Lalli joined us for a cup of mint tea at Ome's home. It was surreal how these mountain folks, with so little access to technology, lived such fulfilling lives. Meanwhile, we city dwellers, surrounded by modern comforts, often found ourselves complaining about trivial things. The simplicity of their existence was a powerful reminder to appreciate the smaller joys of life.

We then took a walk-through apple orchard, eventually arriving at a sage's home. This man was a fascinating blend of the old and new—muscular, with a long beard, and yet possessing a new-age sensibility. His room was filled with unusual items—a guitar, dumbbells, and branded goods. He was a gym trainer by profession, but his journey had led him to become a sadhu. He revealed how, despite his material success, his life had felt empty until he found profound inspiration in Osho's teachings. These teachings led him to leave behind his mundane life and embrace a life of nature and spirituality.

He found his purpose in the village, helping people with his knowledge of physiology and medicine. His ashram was established after a student's family gave him a house. The villagers saw him as a guide, a bridge between the modern world and their ancient ways. As we sat with him, BKji suggested I gift him my book Panchkedar and Badrinath. He was delighted and promised to provide feedback. Before we left, we plucked fresh apples and grapes, savoring the natural sweetness of the fruits.

Returning to Kisan's home, we were treated to a bonfire. The fire crackled, lighting up the cold night and warming our hearts. The light danced on our faces, and the warmth spread deep within. Kisan's children sang songs, and despite our best attempts, we could never quite match their natural rhythm. In the mountains, singing is in the blood, a talent nurtured by the land itself.

We enjoyed tandoori corn and a special dinner, which included local dishes like apple chutney, ghee, Siddu, and Afghani Bolani. Every bite was a reminder of the simple joys of mountain life—delicious, hearty, and full of love.

A Journey Full Circle
Farewell to Galincha, A Bond Eternal

The day had arrived when we would finally part ways, but not before making one last effort to ensure a smooth and timely departure. The previous day, we had discussed when to leave for Chandigarh airport, considering the unpredictable mountain terrain. A single mishap could throw off our schedule and leave us stuck in traffic, ruining the whole day. So, we woke up with an electric sense of anticipation, knowing we would soon be reunited with our families.

Until that morning, we had all wondered why Kisan had bought those traditional Kullu hats (Topi) for us. It turned out, he had kept them for this very day—to offer them to us as a gesture of deep respect and to give us something that would forever remind us to return to this place. The love and warmth we had received from Kisan and his family had touched us deeply, and these hats were the perfect symbol of that bond.

We set off at 5 a.m., Kisan's elder daughter joining us on the journey. Kisan had done so much to make us feel at home during our stay, and now, as we embarked on the challenging drive to Chandigarh, I couldn't help but notice the exhaustion in his eyes. I could see the strain and fatigue from the long days of trekking and hosting. I thought about offering to let him take a break, but with the unpredictable weather and road conditions, I feared it might delay us and cause us to miss our flight.

As dawn broke and the stars faded into the early morning sky, I asked Kisan if I could take over the wheel for a while. Kisan, perhaps unconsciously caught in the Ben Franklin Effect—a psychological phenomenon where asking someone for a favor makes them feel more obligated to help you later —agreed immediately. He settled into the back seat, his daughter resting peacefully on his lap, and we were off. With -

Google Maps guiding us, the drive was smooth and uneventful. We had the express highway before us, and there was no traffic to slow us down.

By 12:30 p.m., we finally entered Chandigarh. The city seemed like a world away from the rugged mountains we had just left. As we made our way to the airport, we asked Kisan's daughter, Jothi, if she wanted anything before, we left. Without hesitation, she smiled and said, "Pizza!" It made us laugh—no matter how remote the place, the influence of Raffaele Esposito's creation had reached even here.

With plenty of time before our flight, we decided to stop at a mall in Chandigarh for lunch at Haldirams. We shared a meal and bought sweets to bring back to our families as a small token of appreciation for all the support they'd given us during this journey. We arrived at the airport around 5:30 p.m., and the reality of departure started to set in. Saying goodbye was like being caught between a rock and a hard place. Leaving behind the people with whom we had formed such a deep, almost divine connection was incredibly difficult.

As we stood there, Kisan's emotions overcame him. Tears rolled down his cheeks as he struggled to say goodbye, and in that moment, it hit us all—we were not just a group of trekkers and villagers; we were one soul, connected in ways that went beyond the physical. The bond we had formed on this journey would never be broken, and we knew we would carry it with us forever, no matter where life took us next.

A Rewarding Trek
The Call of the Shrikhand

The majestic Himalayas, with their awe-inspiring grandeur, stand as timeless sentinels, offering a panoramic embrace of serene snow-clad peaks, diverse flora and fauna, and an atmosphere brimming with tranquility and untamed beauty. This natural paradise captivates the hearts of all, from nature lovers seeking solace in its pristine landscapes to adventure seekers drawn by its exhilarating challenges. Beyond its physical allure, the region is steeped in historical and mythological significance, making it a sacred pilgrimage for devotees and a thrilling haven for trekkers worldwide. The Shrikhand Mahadev trek, though demanding, is a journey like no other, one that immerses you in the profound splendor of the mountains. It's an experience that every soul should embrace at least once in a lifetime, as it offers not only a physical challenge but a deeper connection to nature and spirit.

Trek Details:
Our Tour and Trek Route:
Chandigarh – Shimla - Narkhanda – Hatu Mata Temple – Rampur – Nirmand – Bagipul – Jaon (Trek Inception point) - Singhad (3 km from Jaon) – Barhati Nala (7-8 km from Singhad)– Dandi Dhar – Thachru (4 km from Barhati Nala)– Kali Top – Kunsa (5-6 km from Tachru) – Bheem Dhwari (3 km from Kunsa) - Parvati Bagh (2km from Bheem Dhwari) – Nayan Sarovar - Shrikhand Mahadev Kailash (5-6 kms from Parvati bagh)
Duration: 7-8 days
Altitude: 5200 meters (17,060 feet)
Distance: 65 to 70 kms
Trek Difficulty level: Moderate to Difficult
Location: Kullu, Himachal Pradesh, India

A Gallery Page